CW00839717

300

Crazy
Tennis
Facts

For Tennis Fans

Tennis is believed to have originated in the monastic cloisters in northern France in the 12th century.

The word "Tennis" comes from the Anglo-Norman term "Tenez."

Wimbledon, or the Wimbledon Championships, is the oldest tennis tournament in the world, and also considered to be the most prestigious.

Robin Soderling is the first player to beat Nadal at Roland Garros.

The first Wimbledon was played in 1877. It is also the first of the four "Grand Slams" to be founded.

A player is said to have won a Career Grand Slam if they win all four majors at any time during their career; a Non calendar-Year Grand Slam if they win the four majors consecutively, but not in the same year, and a Grand Slam if they win all four majors in a single year.

The longest tennis match took 11 hours and 5 minutes to complete. It was played between John Isner and Nicolas Mahut.

Tennis is also an Olympic sport, and it can be played by wheelchair users.

The Davis Cup dates to 1900. It is an annual competition between men's national teams.

The Fed Cup, which is an analogous competition for women's national teams, was founded in 1963 to celebrate the 50th anniversary of the ITF.

The year 1968 marked the beginning of the open era in professional tennis.

The tiebreaker, or tiebreak, was invented by James Van Alen in 1965.

The Davis cup first adopted the tiebreaker in all sets except the final set in 1989, and made amendments in their rules to adopt the tiebreakers for all five sets in 2016.

The French Open is the only major tournament to not use a tiebreak in the final set for singles.

Don Budge is the only male player in tennis history to have won six consecutive Grand Slam singles titles, from Wimbledon in 1937 to the US Open in 1938.

The fastest serve in men's tennis came from the racket of Australian Sam Groth at 263.44 km/h.

Germany's Sabine Lisicki hit a serve 210 km/h—the fastest ever recorded in women's tennis.

In 2007, the prize money for Wimbledon winners became equal for men and women.

1968 was the first ever Wimbledon to offer prize money.

Margaret Court has 24 singles majors.

Rafael Nadal holds the most grand slam titles with 21 titles.

If the ball hits a player's body or any part of their clothing before it lands, it is their opponent's point.

Arthur Ashe was the first African American to win the US Open. He won the tournament for the first and the only time in 1968.

The average age of Ball Boys/Girls who serve at Wimbledon is 15. Every year, 250 of these young kids are selected to serve at the tournament.

A Harris Hawk named Rufus is stationed at Wimbledon to keep its sky clear of local pigeons.

Players must submit their clothing to the All England Lawn Tennis and Croquet Club for approval before participating in the Wimbledon championships.

The game of Tennis also became an indirect reason for the death of King James I of Scotland.

Every year, 24 tons of strawberries are consumed during Wimbledon.

In the earlier years of Wimbledon, women wore full-length dresses.

Ivo Karlovic has scored the most aces of all time with 13,599 aces.

1972 is the year when The Association of Tennis Professionals was formed.

As per The International Tennis Federation, the weight of a tennis ball must be between 56.0 and 59.4 grams.

Tennis balls were originally white. In 1986, yellow balls were first introduced at Wimbledon.

Most tennis clubs will require you to wear short-sleeved cotton tops and matching tennis shorts.

Until 1975, three of the four Grand Slams — Wimbledon, the US Open and the Australian Open were played on grass.

Hard courts were used in official tournaments as far back as the 1940s.

Clay, Hard, Glass, Carpet, and Wood are the five types of court surfaces used in professional tennis.

The overall permissible length of a tennis racket is 29 inches.

At Wimbledon, the grass is cut to a height of exactly 8mm during the event.

An estimated 54,250 tennis balls are used during Wimbledon.

Goran İvanisevic is the only Wimbledon winner whose name alternates consonants and vowels.

Boris Becker is the youngest player ever to win a Wimbledon title at 17 years old in 1985.

The shortest tennis match lasted a 20 minutes. İt was played between Susan Tutt and Marion Bandy in 1969 at Wimbledon.

The Roland Garros Stadium, which hosts the French Open, is named after a French aviator Roland Garros.

The winner's trophy at Wimbledon remains on display at the All England Club's museum as winners do not take their trophies with them.

The golden cup given to the men's winner dates back to 1887, while the trophy given to women, called the "salver," dates back to 1864.

Tanking is a term in tennis for losing a match or "fixing" it for some benefit.

Tennis elbow is an inflammation of the tendons that join the forearm muscles on the outside of the elbow.

The loudest grunt, which reached 105 decibels, came from Maria Sharapova in 2009 during Wimbledon.

The first set of sisters to ever win Olympic gold medals in tennis were Venus and Serena Williams.

The Olympics introduced tennis in 1896 and removed the game in 1924. However, tennis was reintroduced at the 1988 Olympics and continues to be a part of the games to this day.

Tennis courts were hourglass-shaped. Rectangular courts have been in existence since 1875.

The International Tennis Federation is the governing body of Tennis and looks after the rules of the game.

For singles matches, the tennis court is 78 feet (23.77 m) long and 27 feet (8.23 m) wide. For doubles matches, the length of the court remains the same but the width is 36 feet (10.97 m).

The service lines are 21 feet from the net on each side.

The lines at the ends of the court are called baselines and the lines at the sides of the court are called side lines.

Wimbledon is the only Grand Slam to have always been played on the same surface — grass.

Grass court is the fastest type of the courts in common use. It tends to favour serve and volley tennis players.

Roger Federer has won a record of eight Wimbledon titles.

Clay court supports baseline players because the court surface allows higher bounce and hence the players get more time to get to the ball and return the shot.

An advantage of the hard court is that it dries up very quickly and hence it is considered an all weather surface.

If an additional ball enters the court while a point is in progress, the point must be replayed.

The receiving opponent is allowed to stand anywhere during the serve except in the service box.

If a doubles team audibly communicates loudly during a point, they forfeit the point.

If the serving player swings during the toss and misses the ball, it is considered a fault.

The world's oldest tennis court is still in use today called the Royal Tennis Court located in Hampton Court Palace, London and dates back to 1526.

The origins of the 15, 30, 40 scoring system are lost in the records of time, but the explanation most commonly given is that they were based on a clock face at one end of the court.

Jimmy Connors has won the US Open on three different surfaces.

Kyrgios is the second player after Lleyton Hewitt who beat Roger Federer, Nadal and Novak Djokovic in their first meeting.

In 1907, Austrian tennis player, Mita Klima became the youngest player to have ever played at Wimbledon. She was 13 years old when she participated in the prestigious tournament.

The tennis ball only stays in play for 20 minutes in a standard match.

There's a pineapple on top of the Wimbledon trophy. Apparently it represents the tradition of English sailors putting pineapples on their gateposts when they returned from a long voyage.

A Grand Slam final once finished in 34 minutes between Steffi Graf and Natasha Zvereva in the French Open Final in 1988.

The longest match on record took place in 2010 at Wimbledon, when John Isner and Nicolas Mahut played over three days which lasted 11 hours and 5 minutes.

It was only in 2007 that prize money for Wimbledon winners became equal for men and women.

Tennis was initially played with your hands. It was called "jeu de paume" (game of the palm). Racquets were introduced in the 16th century.

Real Tennis was being introduced in England in the early 15th century, but it wasn't until the reign of Henry VIII that the game became popular as well.

Two local doctors decided to open up the first tennis club in the world on Avenue Road in Leamington, Warwickshire, England.

The first winner Wimbledon, Spencer Gore, was the first-ever player to use the volley technique.

The Davis Cup is the most important tennis tournament between national teams. The first time it was held was way back in 1900 and it's held every single year.

Dwight Davis is the creator of the Davis Cup. He created the cup when he was just 21 years old and was a tennis player as well.

The rules that had been laid out by the International Tennis Federation in 1924 haven't seen any major changes up until today, except the tiebreak system.

The Hawkeye system was invented by a young British computer expert Paul Hawkins, and was launched in 2001.

There's an International Tennis Hall of Fame in Rhode Island.

Novak Djokovic has a total prize money earnings of $154,833,296.

The strings of the tennis racket were made of cow and sheep guts in the past.

Boris Becker and Stefan Edberg met in three consecutive Wimbledon finals in 1988, 1989 and 1990.

Rafael Nadal has won the French open a record 13 times.

Andy Murray has won 2 gold medals (2012 and 2016).

Andy Murray became a professional tennis player in 2005. He won his first Association of Tennis Professionals title, the SAP Open, in California a year later.

Roger Federer beat Mark Philippoussis to claim his first Wimbledon title in 2003.

Steffi Graf is the only player to achieve a Golden Slam. (Winning all four Grand Slams and an Olympic gold in the same calendar year)

Serena and Venus Williams played each other in four consecutive Grand Slam finals between 2002 and 2003.

Centre Court at Wimbledon has a capacity of 14,979.

Players in a tennis game know that scoring points by hitting the ball just over the net cord is a cheap way to get ahead in the game, so they apologize for hitting the net to acknowledge this.

A type of serve is called a let when the ball hits the net cord but still lands in the service court.

Nick Kyrgios' highest ATP ranking is 13th.

Yellow felt is used in official competitions as the material to cover tennis balls.

Serena Williams has won 23 grand slams whilst her sister Venus Williams has won 7.

Novak Djokovic turned professional in 2003.

Andy Murray faced Novak Djokovic in 7 finals between 2011 and 2016 only winning 2 against the Serbian.

Wheelchair tennis player Esther Vergeer has won 48 grand slam tournaments combining singles and doubles.

The US Open is held in New York City, USA.

Lili Alvarez in 1931, was the first woman to wear shorts in a match at Wimbledon.

Since 1988 the Australian Open has been hosted in Melbourne.

87 million people around the world play tennis. 22% of these are from China, and 20% are from the USA.

47% of global tennis players are female.

The International Tennis Federation collected data to state that 195 nations play the sport of Tennis.

John McEnroe won 4 U.S. Open singles titles.

Rod Laver was nicknamed 'The Rocket'.

Rye Grass is the traditional grass used for Wimbledon.

Ivan Lendl kept sawdust in his pocket during tennis matches.

The traditional day off
for Wimbledon is known
as Middle Sunday.

Billie Jean King won an
incredible 20 Wimbledon titles
and 13 U.S. Open titles.

Rafael Nadal is famous
for his unique Capri Pants
fashion on the court.

Ladies singles events were
first introduced at
Wimbledon in 1884.

Peng Shaui became the first Chinese player to rise to No.1 in February 2014.

Venus Williams lost 5 consecutive grand slam finals to her sister Serena Williams.

The moving roof on Centre Court weighs 1000 tons.

28000 Champagne bottles were consumed in 2015 at the major championships.

In 1968 the winner of the men's singles at Wimbledon received £2000.

In 2016, Murray made three Grand Slam finals, and went on to win Wimbledon for the second time. He also won a second Olympic gold medal in 2016 at the Rio Olympic Games, becoming the first player ever to receive two consecutive gold medals for singles.

Goran Ivanisevic is the only wild card to win the men's singles championship.

The title given to the ladies singles champion at Wimbledon is known as 'The Rosewater Dish'.

The All England Lawn Tennis championship was originally set up to play Croquet.

A tie break occurs when the score is tied at 6-6.

Bjorn Borg won 5 consecutive Wimbledon singles titles between 1976-1980.

Chris Evert won 18 grand slam titles.

Tim Henman won 11 ATP singles titles.

Michael Chang won the 1989 French Open aged 17.

Roger Federer completed the career Grand Slam in 2009.

ATP stands for Association of Tennis Professionals.

A let is when the ball hits the net cord when serving but it still lands in the service court.

The U.S. Open is the 4th and last grand slam to be played each year.

In 1987 The Australian Open was played on grass for the last time.

Serena Williams won her first major tennis championship in 1999.

Rafael Nadal suffered only 3 defeats at Roland Garros.

Iga Swiatek has become the first Pole and the 28th woman to top the world tennis rankings.

Jimmie Conors is the tennis player with the most titles won on the ATP Tour (109).

Novak Djokovic is the player with the most weeks spent on the first world of the ATP list (365).

Djokovic won his first ATP title at the Dutch Open in Amersfoort in 2005.

Novak Djokovic is the only active player to beat Nadal at Roland Garros.

David Nalbandian, Novak Djokovic and Boris Becker are the only three players to beat the top 3 tennis players in one tournament.

Nadal won his first ATP singles title at the Prokom Open in 2004.

Teenage prodigy Emma Raducanu won her maiden Grand Slam title fewer than three months on from her wildcard entry to Wimbledon as the world number 338.

On 29 April 2002, in his hometown of Mallorca and at 15 years and 10 months of age, Nadal won his first ATP match by defeating Ramón Delgado.

Novak Djokovic and Roger Federer won 20 Grand Slam titles each.

The Fed Cup, a women's national team competition named after celebrated tennis player Billie Jean King.

The United States has the most titles won in the Davis Cup (32).

The United States has the most titles won in the Billie Jean King Cup (18).

Chris Evert has the most titles won in the Billie Jean King Cup (8).

The Czech Republic dominated the Fed Cup in the 2010s, winning six of ten competitions in the decade.

The men's equivalent of the Billie Jean King Cup is the Davis Cup, and the Czech Republic, Australia, Russia and the United States are the only countries to have held both Cups at the same time.

In 1919, Hazel Hotchkiss Wightman had an idea for a women's team tennis competition. This was not adopted but she persisted, presenting a trophy at the 1923 annual contest between the United States and Great Britain, named the Wightman Cup.

The first Federation Cup had attracted 16 entry teams, despite no prize money and teams having to pay their own expenses.

For the 1992, a regional group qualifying format was introduced in Fed Cup.

While many nations enter the Fed Cup each year, only 16 countries qualify for the elite World Group and World Group II each year (eight in World Group and eight in World Group II).

The United States has 7 consecutive titles in the Fed Cup (1976- 1982).

The oldest player to play in the Fed Cup is Gill Butterfield from Bermuda who was 52 years old.

The youngest player to play in the Fed Cup is Denise Panagopoulou from Greece who was 12 years old.

The Davis Cup began in 1900 as a challenge between Great Britain and the United States. By 2016, 135 nations entered teams into the competition.

Australia, Russia, the Czech Republic, and the United States are the only countries to have won both Davis Cup and Fed Cup titles in the same year.

The Davis Cup allowed only amateurs and national registered professional players (from 1968) to compete until 1973, five years after the start of the Open Era.

International competitions had been staged for some time before the first Davis Cup match in 1900. From 1892, England and Ireland had been competing in an annual national-team-based competition.

The first match in the Davis Cup, between the United States and Britain (competing as the "British Isles"), was held at the Longwood Cricket Club in Boston, Massachusetts in 1900.

The Davis Cup competition was initially played as a challenge cup. All teams competed against one another for the right to face the previous year's champion in the final round.

Emma Raducanu made history in her Wimbledon debut — becoming the youngest British woman ever to make the tournament's Round of 16.

Up until 1973, the Davis Cup had only ever been won by the United States, Great Britain/British Isles, France and Australia/Australasia. Their domination was eventually broken in 1974 when South Africa and India made the final.

All contract professionals were not allowed to play in the Davis Cup until 1973.

The new format of Davis Cup, backed by footballer Gerard Piqué and Japanese businessman Hiroshi Mikitani, was likened to a world cup of tennis and was designed to be more attractive to sponsors and broadcasters.

After the 2008—2009 Israel—Gaza conflict, 6,000 people protested against Israel outside the Malmö city Davis Cup match between Sweden and Israel in March 2009.

The match between Sweden and Rhodesia in the Davis Cup 1968 was supposed to be played in Båstad but was moved to Bandol, France, due to protests against the Rhodesian white minority government of Ian Smith.

The 18 best national teams are assigned to the World Group and compete annually for the Davis Cup.

Harry Hopman has 16 titles as captain of Australia in the Davis Cup.

The youngest player to play in the Davis Cup is Marco De Rossi from San Marino who was 13 years old.

The oldest player to play in the Davis Cup is Vittorio Pellandra from San Marino who was 66 years old.

Leander Paes has the most years played in the Davis Cup (30).

Although she only plays at the lower levels of the pro tennis circuit, Gail Falkenberg, who is still playing tennis at the age of 71, is the oldest tennis player in the world.

Martina Hingis, was the youngest tennis player in the the "open" era to win a Grand Slam singles title and the youngest to be ranked world number one.

At the 1997 Australian Open, Martina Hingis became the youngest ever Grand Slam champion, winning the tournament aged 16.

Lottie Dod was a five-time champion and is the youngest ever winner of the Wimbledon ladies' singles championships (15 years and 285 days).

The crown for youngest Grand Slam winner, man or woman, belongs to Martina Hingis. In 1997, at the age of 16-years and 117-days, the Swiss defeated former world No. 3 Mary Pierce in the final of the Australian Open.

Roger Federer has won 103 ATP singles titles, the second most of all time after Jimmy Connors.

Roger Federer has finished as the year-end No. 1 five times.

Roger Federer has the record of 237 consecutive weeks at No. 1

Roger Federer is the holder of the most ATP Finals titles, having lifted the trophy a total of six times.

Roger Federer and Stan Wawrinka led the Switzerland Davis Cup team to their first title in 2014.

Roger Federer won the Stefan Edberg Sportsmanship Award 13 times.

Roger Federer is married to former Women's Tennis Association player Miroslava Federer (née Vavrinec), whom he met while they were both competing for Switzerland at the 2000 Sydney Olympics.

Roger Federer won his first ATP match in Toulouse against Guillaume Raoux in 1998.

Federer's first singles win was at the 2001 Milan Indoor tournament, where he defeated Julien Boutter in the final.

In 2001, Federer made his first Grand Slam quarterfinal at the French Open, losing to former world No. 2 and eventual finalist Alex Corretja.

Roger Federer international breakthrough came at the 2001 Wimbledon Championships, where the 19-year-old Federer faced the four-time defending champion and all-time Grand Slam leader Pete Sampras.

Roger Federer speaks Swiss German, German, French, and English fluently.

Roger Federer has won Roland Garros only one time.

Roger Federer has a total prize money earnings of $ 130, 594,339.

Novak Djokovic has finished as the year-end No. 1 a record seven times.

Roger Federer won his first Master Series event at the 2002 Hamburg Masters on clay, over Marat Safin; the victory put him in top 10 for the first time.

Novak Djokovic has won 86 ATP titles (5th in the Open Era).

In August 2020, Djokovic and Vasek Pospisil announced the formation of the Professional Tennis Players Association as the first player-only association in tennis.

Djokovic is the only man to complete a non-calendar year Grand Slam and the first man in the Open Era to achieve a double career Grand Slam.

Djokovic is the only player to complete the career Golden Masters on the ATP Tour, which he has done twice.

At age 20, Djokovic disrupted Roger Federer's and Rafael Nadal's streak of 11 consecutive majors.

Novak Djokovic has won his first Grand Slam title at the 2008 Australian Open.

By 2010, Djokovic also separated himself from the rest of men's tennis to join Federer and Nadal in the Big Three, the group of three players who have dominated men's tennis for more than a decade.

Djokovic has won a record 37 titles in the ATP Masters tournaments.

Djokovic won the 2016 French Open to complete the first and only non-calendar year Grand Slam in the Open Era and his first career Grand Slam.

Djokovic was the first man since Rod Laver in 1969 to hold all four major titles at once and the only one in history to do so on three different surfaces.

Djokovic has won the Laureus World Sportsman of the Year award four times.

Former Croatian tennis players Ivan Ljubicic and Goran Ivanisevic are the coaches of Roger Federer and Novak Djokovic.

Two younger brothers of Novak Djokovic, Marko and Djordje, have also played professional tennis.

Djokovic is a self-described fan of languages, speaking Serbian, English, French, German, and Italian.

Djokovic first tour-level tournament was Umag in 2004, where he lost to Filippo Volandri in the round of 32.

Nadal has won 21 Grand Slam men's singles titles, the most in history, including a record 13 French Open titles.

Nadal's 81 consecutive wins on clay is the longest single-surface win streak in the Open Era.

Nadal was one of the most successful teenagers in ATP Tour history, reaching No. 2 in the world and winning 16 titles before his 20th birthday.

After defeating Novak Djokovic at the 2010 US Open final, then 24-year-old Nadal became the youngest man in the Open Era to achieve the career Grand Slam, and the first man to win three Majors on three different surfaces (hard, grass and clay) in the same year.

From 2005 to 2017, Nadal was coached by his uncle Toni Nadal.

Representing Spain, Nadal has won an Olympic gold medal in both singles and doubles, and has contributed to five Davis Cup titles.

Rafael Nadal turned pro in 2001.

Rafael Nadal has 91 career titles.

Ivan Lendl is the third most trophy tennis player with 94 titles.

Nadal defeated Mariano Puerta in the first Roland Garros final, becoming the second man, after Mats Wilander in 1982, to win the French Open on his first attempt.

Nadal was the first male teenager to win a major singles title since Pete Sampras won the 1990 US Open at age 19.

Federer and Nadal have played 40 times. Nadal leads 24—16 overall and 10—4 in Grand Slam tournaments.

Novak Djokovic and Nadal have met 58 times (more than any other pair in the Open Era). Nadal leads 10—7 at Grand Slam events but trails 28—30 overall.

Nadal holds an all-time record of 12 Barcelona Open titles, 11 Monte-Carlo Masters titles, and 10 Rome Masters titles.

Nadal 13 French Open titles are a record at any single tournament, and is the title leader in three major tiers of the ATP Tour (Grand Slam, ATP Masters 1000, ATP 500) in the Open Era.

Nadal's dominance on Clay is reflected by his honorific title as the "King of Clay".

Nadal is one of two male tennis players, along with Agassi, to win the Olympic Singles Gold Medal as well as the four Grand Slams in his career, a feat known as a Career Golden Slam.

Nadal was the first and only player in history to win all three Masters clay court tournaments (Monte-Carlo, Madrid, Rome) and the French Open in a calendar year, a feat known as a "Clay Slam".

In 2020, Nadal became the first player to win the French Open in three different decades.

Despite having several more years being one of the world's best tennis players, Roddick's win in the 2003 U.S. Open is his only Grand Slam triumph.

Nadal holds the Open Era record for the most consecutive seasons winning at least one tournament (19 years) and two tournaments (18 years) respectively.

128036 Rafaelnadal is a main belt asteroid discovered in 2003 at the Observatorio Astronómico de Mallorca and named after Nadal.

Despite being left-handed while playing tennis, Nadal is known for being right-handed while doing things in everyday life such as writing and playing golf.

Federer founded the Laver Cup, which pits Europe against the rest of the world.

Federer and Novak Djokovic have played 50 times, with Federer trailing 23–27.

Federer was ranked among the top eight players in the world continuously for 14 years and two weeks—from 14 October 2002 until 31 October 2016.

On winning the 2009 French Open and completing the career Grand Slam, Federer became the first male tennis player to grace the cover of Sports Illustrated since Andre Agassi in 1999.

Federer has been nicknamed the "Federer Express" (shortened to "Fed Express" or "FedEx").

In 2012, the city of Halle, in Germany, unveiled "Roger-Federer-Allee" in recognition of Federer's success on the grass at the Gerry Weber Open.

In December 2019, Federer became the first living person to be celebrated on Swiss coins.

The gluten-free diet has been credited for improving Djokovic endurance on the court and playing a role in his subsequent success.

Serena Williams has won 23 Grand Slam singles titles, the most by any player in the Open Era, and the second-most of all time (behind Margaret Court's 24).

Along with her older sister Venus, Serena Williams was coached by her parents Oracene Price and Richard Williams.

From the 2002 French Open to the 2003 Australian Open, Serena Williams was dominant, winning all four major singles titles (each time over Venus in the final) to achieve a non-calendar year Grand Slam and the career Grand Slam, known as the "Serena Slam".

Beginning at the 2012 Wimbledon Championships, Serena Williams returned to dominance, claiming Olympic gold and becoming the first tennis player to achieve a Career Golden Slam in both singles and doubles.

Serena Williams has won 14 major women's doubles titles, all with her sister Venus, and the pair are unbeaten in Grand Slam doubles finals.

Serena holds the most combined major titles in singles, doubles, and mixed doubles among active players, with 39: 23 in singles, 14 in women's doubles, and two in mixed doubles.

Billie Jean King is the oldest winner of a singles titles with 39 years, 7 months and 23 days.

Tracy Austin is the the youngest winner of a singles titles with 14 years and 28 days.

Mirjana Lucic Baroni has the longest gap between two titles– 16 years and 4 months.

Serena Williams is the WTA career prize money leader with $94,518,971.

Mirjana Lucic Baroni is the lowest-ranked player(unranked) to win a singles titles.

Martina Navratilova has the most doubles titles won with 177 titles.

Zhang Suai is the lowest-ranked player(226) to defeat a world No.1 (Dinara Safina).

Serena Williams is the oldest player who was WTA No.1 with 35 years and 224 days.

Martina Hingis is the youngest player who was WTA No.1 with 16 years and 152 days.

Steffi Graf was ranked world No. 1 for a record 377 weeks.

In 1988, Steffi Graf became the first tennis player to achieve the Golden Slam by winning all four major singles titles and the Olympic gold medal in the same calendar year.

Steffi Graf won 107 singles titles.

Steffi Graf and Margaret Court are the only players, female or male, to win three majors in a calendar year five times.

Steffi Graf married former world No. 1 men's tennis player Andre Agassi in October 2001.

At the start of her first full professional year in 1983, Steffi Graf was 13 years old.

Martina Navratilova won 18 Grand Slam singles titles, 31 major women's doubles titles, and 10 major mixed doubles titles, for a combined total of 59 major titles, marking the Open Era record for the most Grand Slam titles won by a single player.

Martina Navratilova reached the Wimbledon singles final 12 times, including for nine consecutive years from 1982 through 1990.

Martina Navratilova won the women's singles title at Wimbledon a record nine times.

Navratilova was WTA world No. 1 in singles for a total of 332 weeks.

Navratilova was WTA world No.1 for a record 237 weeks in doubles, making her the only player, male or female, in history to have held the top spot in both singles and doubles for over 200 weeks.

Navratilova is one of the three female tennis players, along with Margaret Court and Doris Hart, to have accomplished a Career Grand Slam in women's singles and doubles, and mixed doubles, called the career "Grand Slam Boxed Set".

Navratilova won her last major title in 2006, adding the mixed doubles crown at the 2006 US Open to her resume just a few weeks before her 50th birthday, 32 years after her first Major title in 1974.

Originally from Czechoslovakia, Martina Navratilova was stripped of her citizenship when, in 1975 at age 18, she asked the United States for political asylum and was granted temporary residence.

Navratilova won her first professional singles title in Orlando, Florida, in 1974, at the age of 17.

On September 6, 2014, Navratilova proposed to her long-time girlfriend Julia Lemigova, a former Miss USSR, at the US Open.

Chris Evert won 157 singles titles.

Chris Evert reached 34 Grand Slam singles finals, more than any other player in the history of professional tennis.

Evert reached the semifinals or better in 52 of the 56 Grand Slams she played, including the semifinals or better of 34 consecutive Grand Slams entered from the 1971 US Open through the 1983 French Open.

Evert won a record seven titles at the French Open.

By 2010, Murray and Novak Djokovic had separated themselves from the rest of men's tennis, joining Federer and Nadal in the Big Four.

Andy Murray made his major breakthrough in 2012 by defeating Djokovic to win the US Open. With this title, he became the first British Grand Slam singles champion since Virginia Wade in 1977, and the first male champion since Fred Perry in 1936.

Murray defended his title at the 2016 Rio Olympics to become the only man with two Olympic gold medals in singles.

Andy Murray became only the second top 10 player in the history of the ATP Tour to have a female coach when he hired Amélie Mauresmo.

Nicknamed "the happy slam", the Australian Open is the highest attended Grand Slam event, with more than 812,000 people attending the 2020 tournament.

Australian Open was also the first Grand Slam tournament to feature indoor play during wet weather or extreme heat with its three primary courts.

The Australian Open is managed by Tennis Australia, formerly the Lawn Tennis Association of Australia (LTAA), and was first played at the Warehouseman's Cricket Ground in Melbourne in November 1905.

The first winner of Roland Garros was H. Briggs, a Briton who resided in Paris and was a member of the Club Stade Français.

The trophy awarded to the winner of the Roland Garros men's singles is called the Coupe des Mousquetaires (The Musketeers' Cup). It is named in honor of the "Four Musketeers".

The Four Musketeers, named after a 1921 film adaptation of Alexandre Dumas' novel, were French tennis players who were top competitors of the game during the second half of the 1920s and early 1930s, winning 20 Grand Slam titles and 23 Grand Slam doubles.

The American John Isner holds the record for the most aces in a single match. He hit 112 aces in a match against Nicolas Mahut (who himself hit 103) in the first round of Wimbledon in 2010.

Back in 1975 on May 26, at the Surrey Grass Court Championships at Surbiton, Anthony Fawcett and Keith Glass racked up a record 37 deuces in a single game for a grand total of 80 points.

The fastest female tennis serve ever recorded 220 km/h (136.7 mph) in 2018 by Georgina Garcia Pérez of Spain.

The highest total of aces in one WTA match on record is 31, set by Kristyna Pliskova in the second round of the 2016 Australian Open.

In tennis, a bagel is when the set ends with a score of 6—0. An extremely rare type of bagel, where no point is lost, is called a golden set.

Rafael Nadal has been bageled 15 times in his entire career, with Roger Federer being the only player to bagel him three times.

In an exhibition match, 14 year old Nadal caught the tennis world by surprise by beating Pat Cash. The 1987 Wimbledon winner was retired at the time, but still playing regularly in numerous events around the world.

Scan The QR Code To Check Out More Utopia Press Books On Amazon!

Printed in Great Britain
by Amazon